Self Portraits
2011-2012

ROWAN MOORE

THESE PAINTINGS WERE FIRST PUBLISHED AS A SMALL EDITION BOOK
IN DECEMBER 2019

COPYRIGHT © 2020 BY ROWAN MOORE
ALL RIGHTS RESERVED. DO NOT REPRODUCE WITHOUT PERMISSION OF THE ARTIST.

ISBN: 9798621195656

MANUFACTURED IN THE UNITED STATES OF AMERICA

PAINTINGS BY ROWAN MOORE
BOOK DESIGN DOUBLEMRANCH.COM

INDEPENDENTLY PUBLISHED

DOUBLEMRANCH.COM

A FAVORITE WES ANDERSON FILM INSPIRED ME TO BEGIN PAINTING SMALL POSTCARD-SIZED SELF PORTRAITS. I WAS THINKING A LOT ABOUT SELFIES AT THE TIME BECAUSE OF THE RISE OF SMARTPHONES AND SOCIAL MEDIA. INSTEAD OF STOPPING AT THE PHOTOGRAPH I TURNED TO THE PLEASURE OF INTERPRETING THE MADE IMAGE IN PAINT. THIS SERIES IS PAINTED USING WATER COLOR FROM PHOTOGRAPHS MADE WITH A SMARTPHONE. SOMETIMES I PAINTED DIRECTLY FROM MY PHONE BUT I ALSO MADE ENLARGEMENTS TO WORK FROM. I EVENTUALLY PAINTED ABOUT 14 OF THESE PORTRAITS IN VARIOUS SIZES.
— ROWAN MOORE

4 X 6 IN

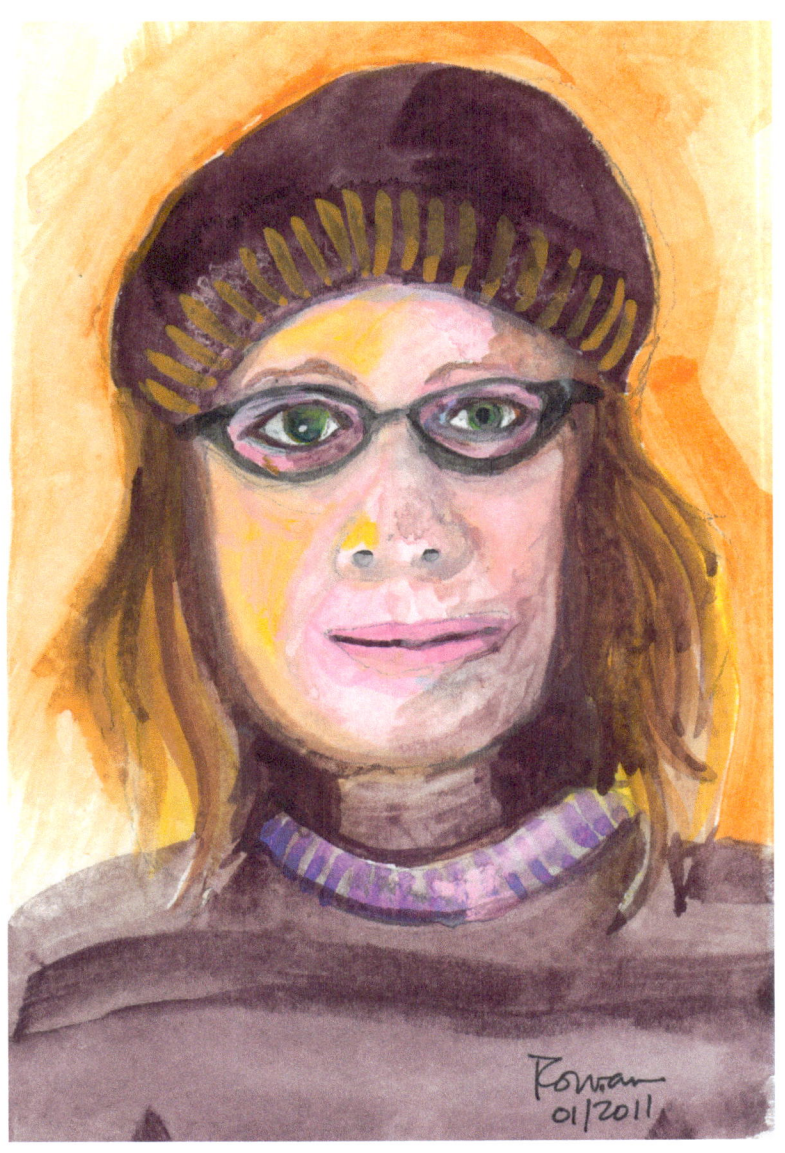

4 X 6 IN

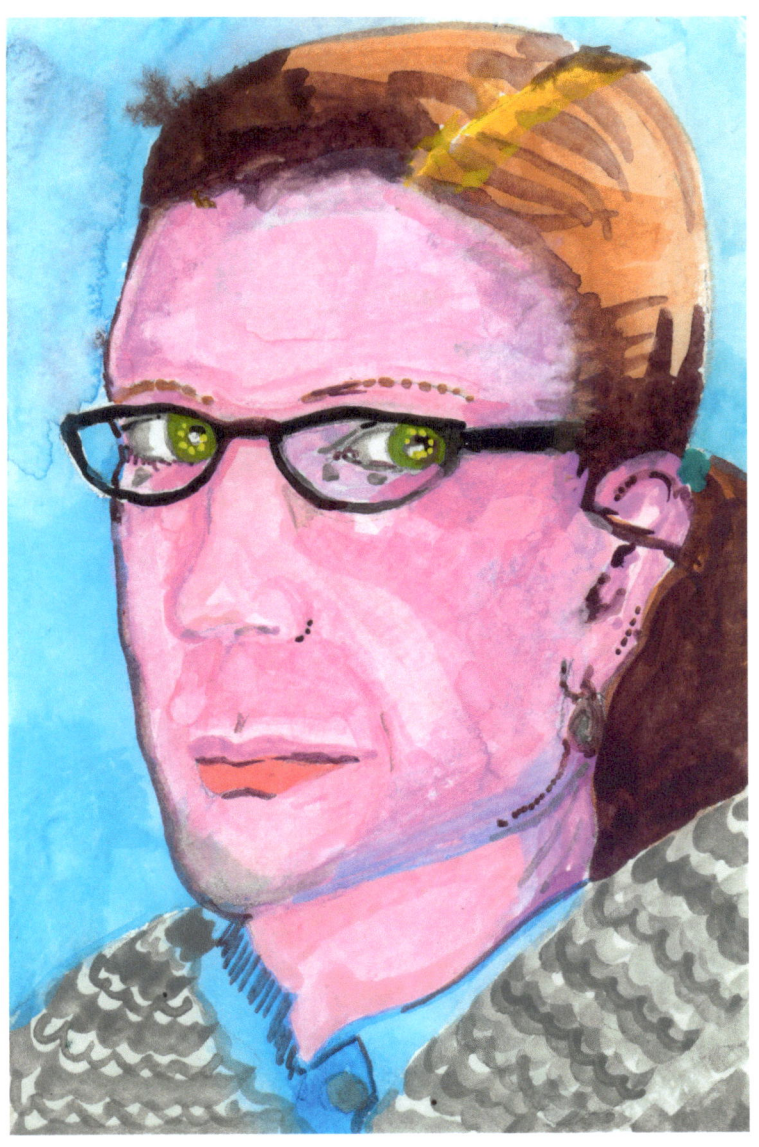

4 X 6 IN

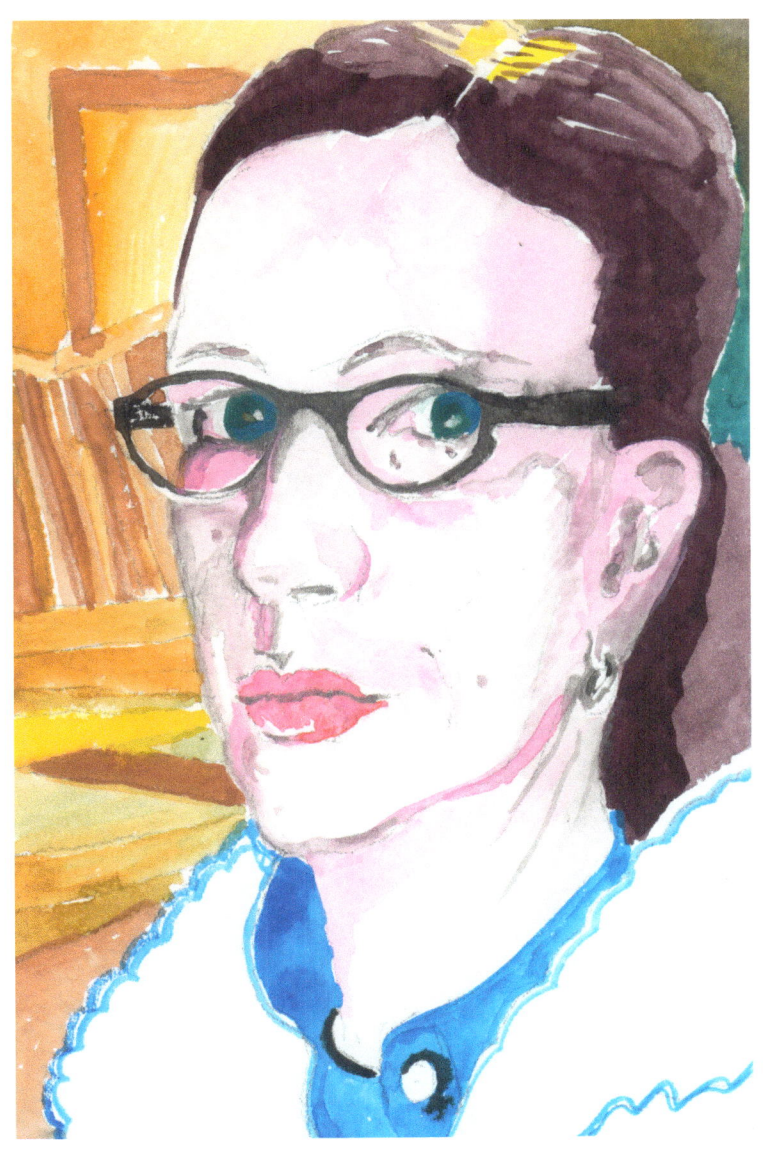

4 X 6 IN

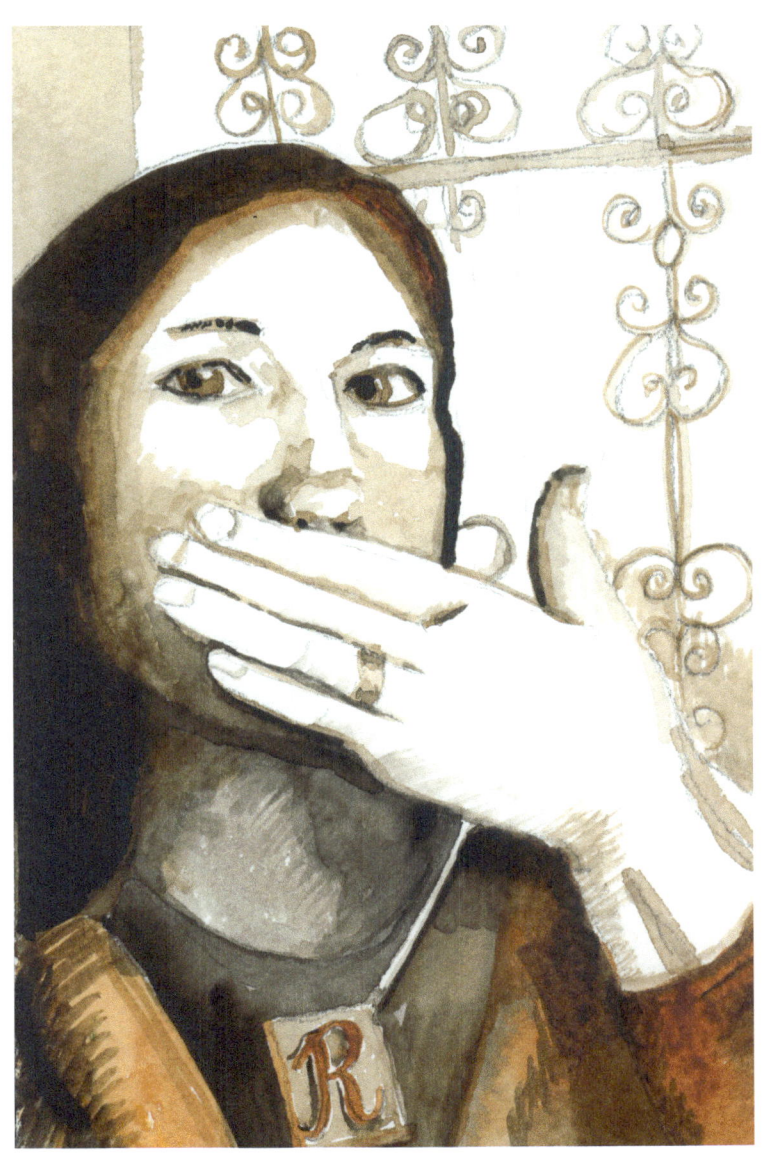

4 X 6 IN

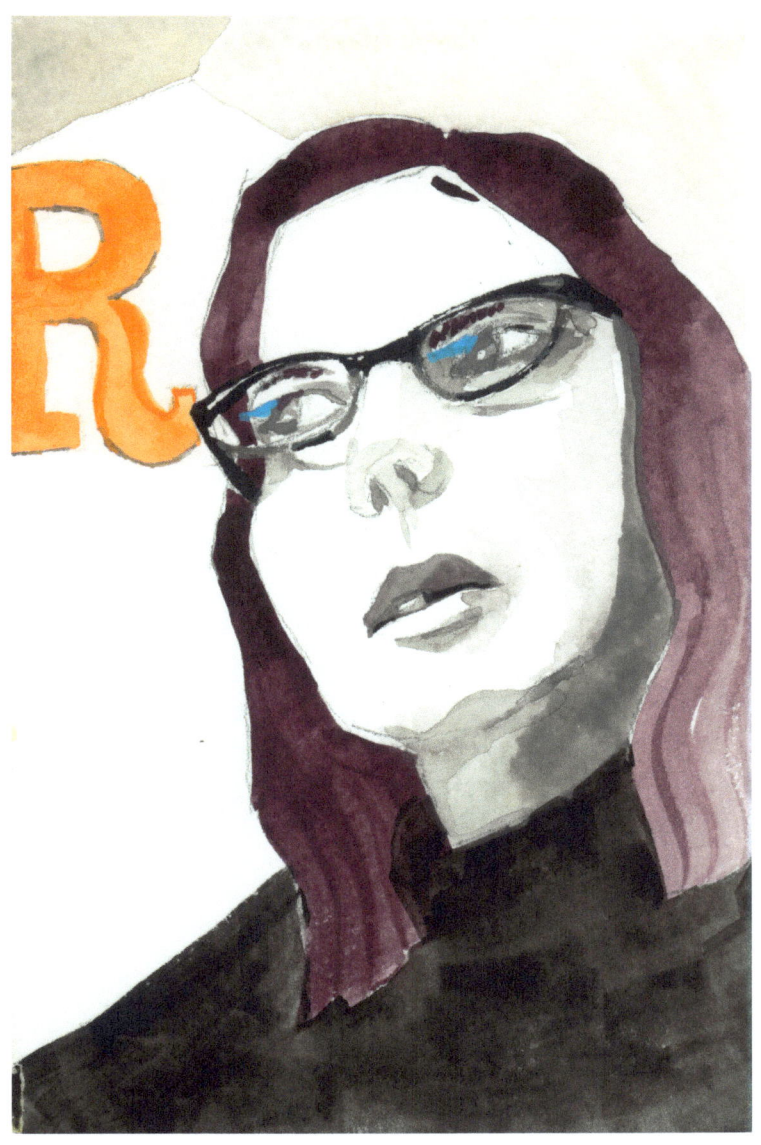

4 X 6 IN

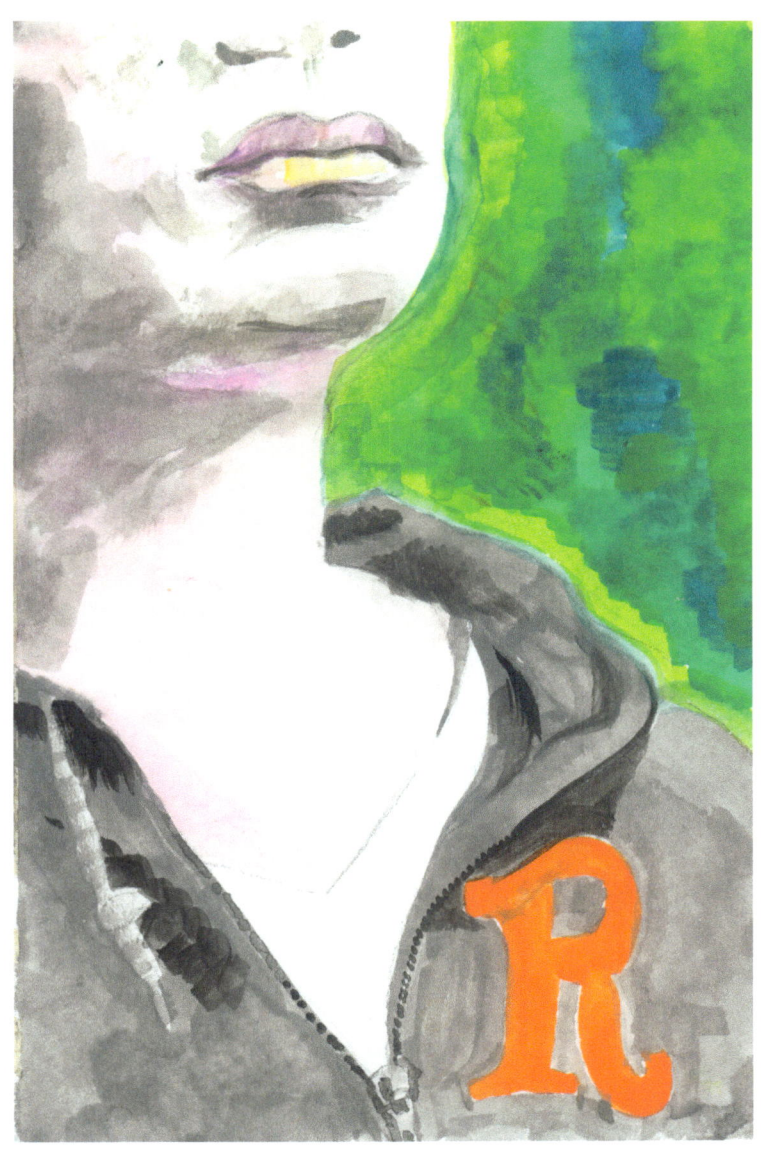

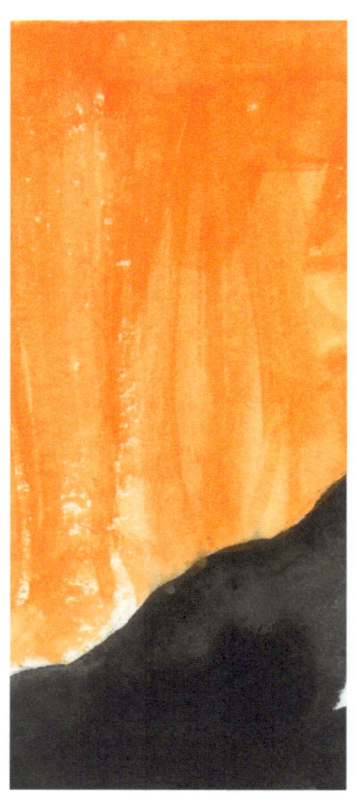

6 X 4 IN

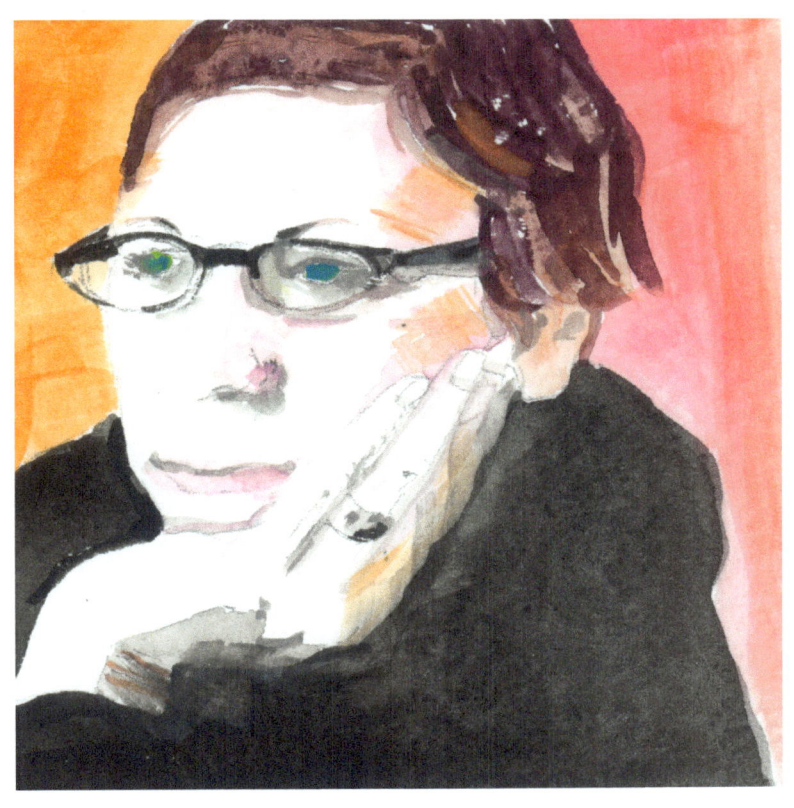

5 X 4.25 IN

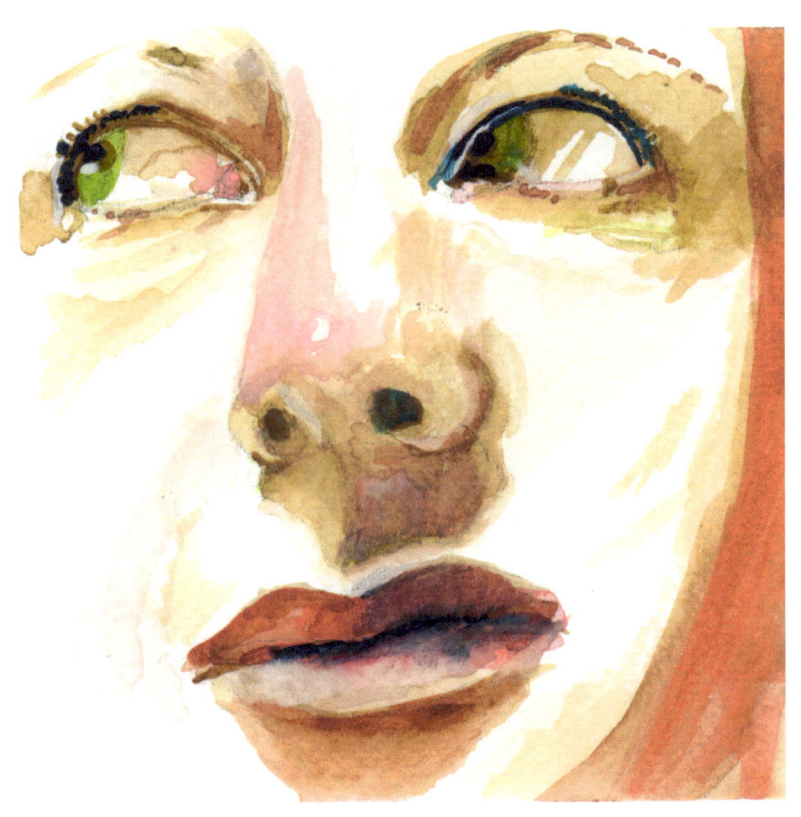

9.5 X 12.5 IN (DETAIL)

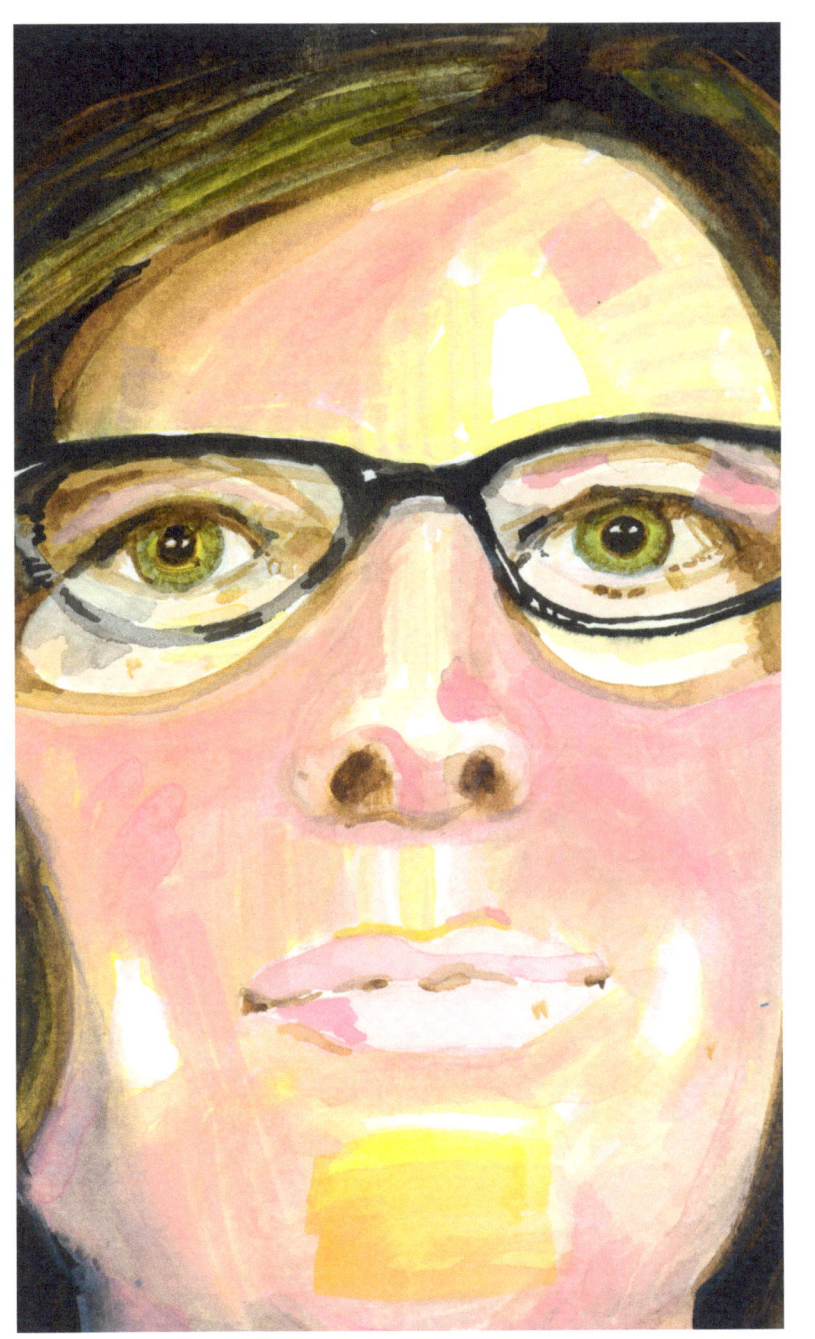

12.5 X 9.5 IN (DETAIL)

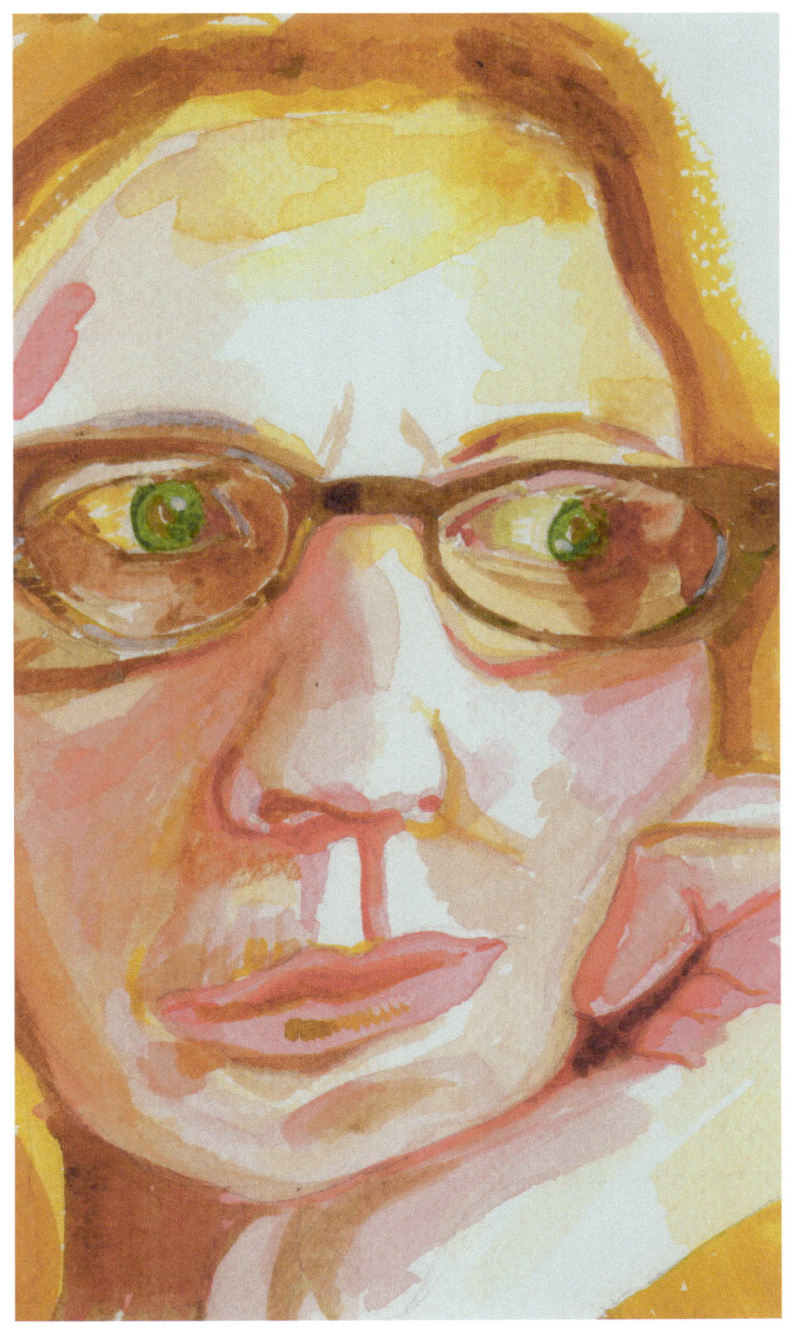

15 X 11 IN (DETAIL)

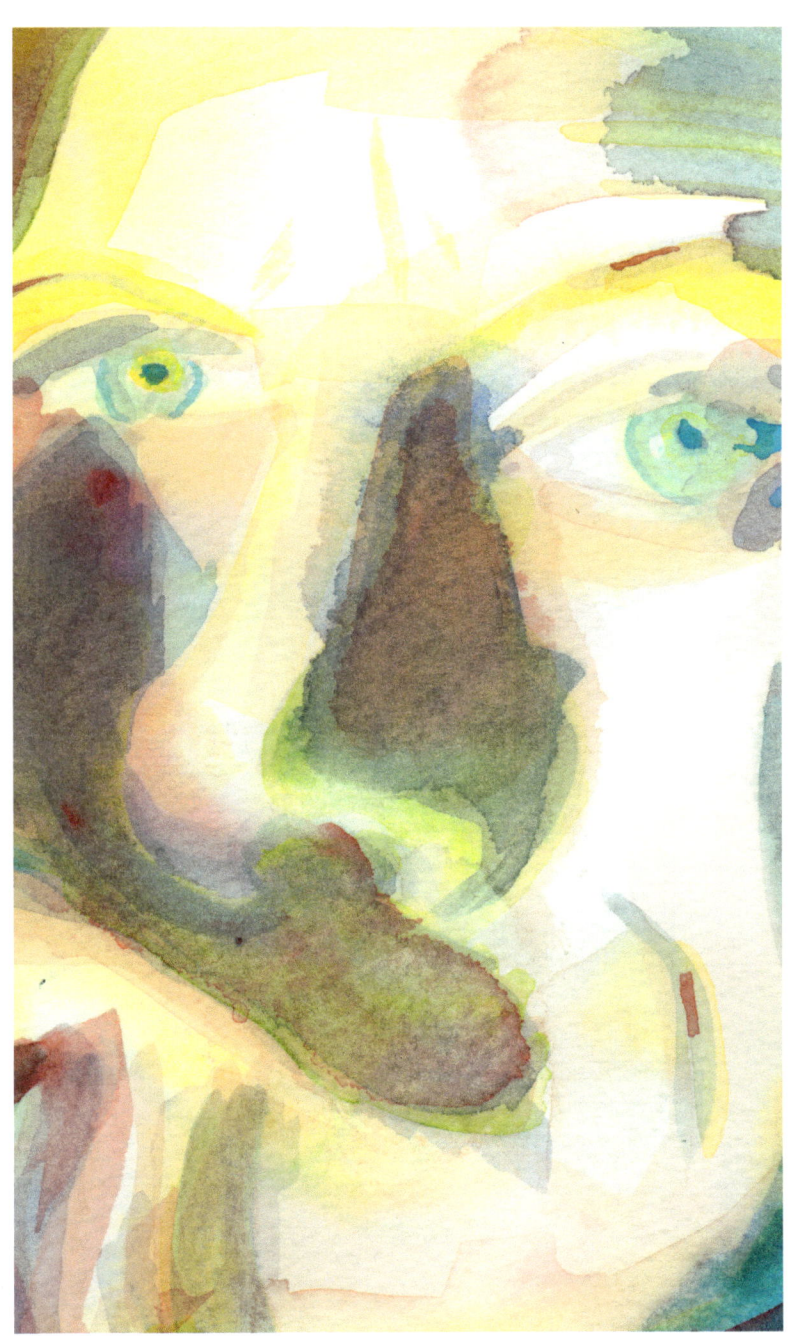

15 X 11 IN

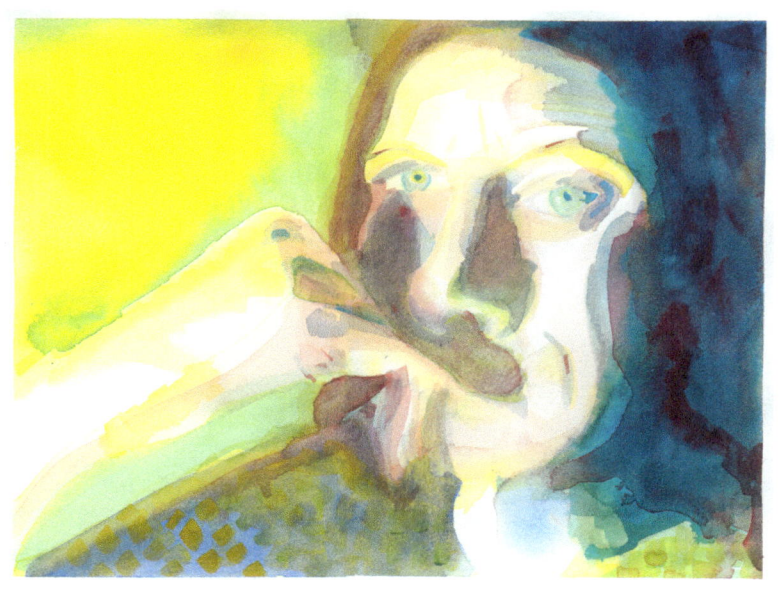

ROWAN MOORE IS A SELF SUSTAINING VISUAL ARTIST PRACTICING IN THE PACIFIC NORTHWEST. SCHOOLED IN BRITISH COLUMBIA AND CALIFORNIA, HER CAREER BEGAN IN THE MUSIC INDUSTRY IN LOS ANGELES. MOVING AHEAD OF THE DIGITAL NEW WAVE AND SEEING THE POTENTIAL TO IMAGINE A CREATIVE PRACTICE OUTSIDE A TRADITIONAL SETTING MOORE LEFT LOS ANGELES IN 1994 AND MOVED ONTO A 5 ACRE PROPERTY NEAR THE CANADIAN BORDER. HERE SHE HAS DEVELOPED AN INTEGRATIVE ART PRACTICE THAT IS FINANCIALLY AND CREATIVELY SUSTAINING.

THIS PROJECT, A COLLECTION OF PAINTINGS GATHERED TOGETHER IN A BOOK FORM IS AN EXPLORATION INTO USING AN AVAILABLE DIGITAL PUBLICATION PLATFORM TO PRODUCE AND DISTRIBUTE CREATIVE WORK. LIFTING A VEIL SO TO SPEAK BETWEEN CREATOR AND AUDIENCE BY REMOVING THE OBSTACLES OF TRADITIONAL PUBLICATION AND DISTRIBUTION CHANNELS. USING A MONOLITHIC DISTRIBUTOR LIKE AMAZON MEANS THE FINANCIAL BURDEN OF PRODUCTION SHIFTS FROM ARTIST TO VIEWER. THE BOOK IS AVAILABLE AS AN E-BOOK AND ALSO AS A PRINT ON DEMAND BOOK.

"IN MY CREATIVE PRACTICE I AM INTERESTED IN ISSUES OF IMPERMANENCE AND SUSTAINABILITY RELATED TO THE OBJECTS I CHOOSE TO CREATE, SELL OR DISTRIBUTE. I WONDER ABOUT THE DIGITAL EXPERIENCE BECOMING A REPLACEMENT FOR LOOKING AT A REAL PAINTING. COULD THERE BE A TIME WHEN ART CAN BE APPRECIATED BY PROXY ALONE. IS THAT WHERE WE ARE HEADED?"
— ROWAN MOORE

www.ingramcontent.com/pod-product-compliance
Lightning Source LLC
Chambersburg PA
CBHW040348220526
45473CB00009B/2816